NOAH
and the
Great Big
BOAT

For my best friend, supporter and encourager, my husband.   A.W.

The original story of Noah comes from the Bible. You can find it in the first book of the Bible,
Genesis, chapter six and verse one, all the way through to chapter nine and verse eighteen.
"...and rain fell on the earth for forty days and forty nights." Genesis 7:12

Text and illustrations copyright © 2019 Antonia Woodward
This edition copyright © 2019 Lion Hudson IP Limited

The right of Antonia Woodward to be identified as the author and the illustrator of this work has been
asserted by her in accordance with the Copyright, Designs and Patents Act 1988.

Published by
Lion Hudson Limited
Wilkinson House, Jordan Hill Business Park
Banbury Road, Oxford OX2 8DR, England
www.lionhudson.com

ISBN 978 0 7459 7681 5

First edition 2019

A catalogue record for this book is available from the British Library

Printed and bound in China, June 2019, LH54

NOAH
and the
Great Big BOAT

Antonia Woodward

LION
CHILDREN'S

When God made the Earth it was a **good** place

full of **love**,
and **beauty**,

and **hope**.

But somehow, over time, it had become a bad place,
a tangled mess of hate, anger, and selfishness.
   God looked down from heaven and saw what
a sad place the Earth had become.

"It's time for a fresh start," he said.

Now, Noah was a good man.

He was kind and peaceful, and he loved God.

God called to him: "Noah, I need your help!
I'm going to wash the Earth clean, and I'd like
you to take care of all the animals while I do."

"But
however
will I
find
them all?"

asked Noah.

"Don't worry, I'll bring them all to you,"
said God, "but first…"

"...I want you to build a Great Big BOAT."

So, Noah and his family set to work.

They hammered…

and they nailed…

and they sawed…

…until the boat was complete.

And on the very day it was finished…

...STAMPEDE!

From the **spottiest** to the stripiest,
the *fastest* to the s l o w e s t,
the LARGEST
down to the very very smallest,

two of every animal on the Earth flocked
to Noah and his Great Big Boat.

Safely inside,
the door
slammed shut,

the clouds gathered…

and it began to rain.

And rain…

and *rain*.

Until eventually…

...the *whole* earth was covered in blue.

For forty days and forty nights it *did* not stop.

The Great Big Boat and all inside floated on.

Then one delightful day…

…there was no more rain!

With great excitement Noah let loose a dove. It flew away, but soon came back. There was nowhere for it to land.

Noah and the animals waited seven days as the waters went down and down and down. Then once again, Noah released the dove.

This time the dove returned with a fresh green leaf.

"Now if there is a leaf,' said Noah,
thoughtfully, "then there is a tree...

and if there is a *tree*

then there is

dry land

for the tree to stand on.

Our floating is nearly over!"

God sent a strong wind to dry up
all the floodwater.

When every last drop had dried up, Noah, his family, and all the animals stepped down onto a
fresh,
clean,
new
Earth.

And God said to them:

"This is a new day! Enjoy the land, settle down, make yourselves at home. I will never cover the Earth with water like this again. Never EVER. When you see a rainbow high up in the clouds, remember this as a sign of my true promise."

And life began again.

Other titles by Antonia Woodward

The Promised One

The Extra Special Baby

The Not-so-very Lost Lamb